D1716341

Reading Essentials® in Science

CHEMISTRY CLUES

Atoms, Molecules, and Compounds

JENNY KARPELENIA

PERFECTION LEARNING®

Editorial Director: Susan C. Thies
Editor: Mary L. Bush
Design Director: Randy Messer
Book Design: Emily J. Greazel
Cover Design: Michael A. Aspengren

A special thanks to the following for his scientific review of the book:
Kristin Mandsager, Instructor of Physics and Astronomy,
North Iowa Area Community College

Image credits:
©Associated Press: p. 10; ©Bettmann/CORBIS: pp. 8, 14, 26 (bottom); ©Kevin
Schafer/CORBIS: p. 17; ©Digital Art/CORBIS: p. 24; ©Charles Mauzy/CORBIS:
p. 26 (top); ©Bernard Annebicque/CORBIS SYGMA: p. 27

Image100: pp. 3, 7; Perfection Learning Corporation: pp. 9, 11, 12, 15, 16, 18, 19,
20, 21, 23 (top), 25; Photos.com: back cover, front cover, pp. 4, 5, 6, 23 (bottom), 29

Text © 2006 by Perfection Learning® Corporation.
All rights reserved. No part of this book may be reproduced, stored in a retrieval
system, or transmitted in any form or by any means, electronic, mechanical,
photocopying, recording, or otherwise, without prior permission of the publisher.
Printed in the United States of America.

For information, contact
Perfection Learning® Corporation
1000 North Second Avenue, P.O. Box 500
Logan, Iowa 51546-0500.
Phone: 1-800-831-4190
Fax: 1-800-543-2745
perfectionlearning.com

1 2 3 4 5 6 PP 10 09 08 07 06 05

Paperback ISBN 0-7891-6617-8
Reinforced Library Binding ISBN 0-7569-4641-7

Contents

CHAPTER 1

Atoms, Atoms, Everywhere

They are everywhere! They make up the air you breathe, the water you drink, and the food you eat. They surround you in your home. They are in your floors, furniture, clothing, and pets. They even make up you and your family. You cannot escape from them. But don't panic. There's no need to worry. What are *they*? They are tiny particles called **atoms**, and they make up everything in the world.

ONLY ONE

Elements are nonliving materials made of only one kind of atom. There are more than 100 known elements in the world today. Some common elements are hydrogen, helium, carbon, oxygen, aluminum, chlorine, iron, copper, and gold. Most elements are found in the ground, water, or air. A few can actually be made in a laboratory. Plutonium, neptunium, and einsteinium are examples of human-made elements.

Tracing the Path of Science

More than 2000 years ago, the ancient Greeks already understood that materials were different from one another and could be broken down into smaller parts. These early thinkers, however, believed that there were only four basic elements—fire, air, water, and earth. It wasn't until the mid-1600s that scientists began determining that there were more than four elements made of just one type of particle.

MORE THAN ONE

The elements are a good start, but obviously there are more than 100 different substances in the world. Where does the rest of the matter come from? Atoms combine to create the millions of materials that make up you and everything around you.

A **molecule** is formed when two or more atoms join together. Molecules can be made from the same type of atoms. For example, when two oxygen atoms stick together, they form oxygen gas (O_2).

Molecules can also be made from different atoms, such as when carbon combines with oxygen to form carbon dioxide gas (CO_2). Molecules formed from different types of atoms (or elements) are called **compounds**. Compounds are formed by **chemical reactions**. A compound doesn't behave in the same way as the individual elements that make it. The compound becomes a new substance with different characteristics.

Water (H_2O) is a compound made up of the elements hydrogen and oxygen. The acid in your stomach that helps break down food is a compound called *hydrochloric acid* (HCl). It is made of the elements hydrogen and chlorine. The salt you sprinkle on your french fries is a compound too. Sodium and chlorine combine to make sodium chloride (NaCl), which is commonly known as table salt.

A Few Hints About Chemical Formulas

A chemical (or molecular) formula is the shorthand way to write the name of a molecule or compound. One or two letters represent each element. The first letter of each element is capitalized. If there's a second letter, it's lowercased. For example, H is the abbreviation for hydrogen, while Cu stands for copper.

If you want to know how many different elements make up a compound, look at the different element symbols in the formula. Remember not to count the same element more than once. For example, the compound $HC_2H_3O_2$ (acetic acid) is made of three elements—hydrogen (H), carbon (C), and oxygen (O).

A subscript is the small number placed below and to the right of a symbol. The subscript represents how many atoms of that element are in one molecule. If there isn't a subscript, it means there's only 1 atom of that element in the molecule. For example, there are 8 atoms in acetic acid ($HC_2H_3O_2$)—4 hydrogen (H), 2 carbon (C), and 2 oxygen (O).

BUILDING THE WORLD ONE ATOM AT A TIME

They are everywhere and in everything. The world would be very empty without the atoms that make up elements, molecules, and compounds. In fact, there would be no world itself since it, too, is made of atoms. Atoms, molecules, and compounds truly are the building blocks of the world.

CHAPTER 2

A Look at the Atom

S o what is it about the atom that makes it the base of all living and nonliving things and allows it to combine with other atoms to form molecules and compounds? Over time, scientists have developed an understanding of this tiny particle's structure and behavior.

Tracing the Path of Science

Scientists' knowledge of the atom has changed throughout history. Around 400 B.C., Greek philosopher Democritus was the first to propose that everything was made of tiny indivisible particles. In the early 1800s, John Dalton was the first modern scientist to confirm and research this idea. He also believed that the particles of one element were different from the particles of other elements. In 1897, J. J. Thomson discovered negatively charged **electrons**. He was the first to suggest that atoms had smaller particles within them. In the early 1900s, Ernest Rutherford experimented with the **nucleus**

Democritus

of atoms and discovered **protons**. He was the first to realize that most of the mass of an atom was in its nucleus. Working with Rutherford, J. Chadwick discovered the **neutron**. Danish physicist Niels Bohr made a major breakthrough when he created a model of the atom with electrons in orbits. The model was made even more complete in 1924 when Louis de Broglie (pronounced dee BROY) added his knowledge of how electrons moved from one energy level to the next. This led to the modern model and theory of the atom.

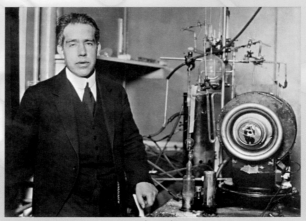

Niels Bohr

WHAT'S INSIDE?

An atom has a center called a *nucleus*. Inside the nucleus are tiny particles called *protons* and *neutrons*.

Protons are positively charged particles. Each element's atom has a unique number of protons in its nucleus. These protons give an element its physical properties. Each proton has a mass of nearly one atomic mass unit (amu).

Neutrons are neutral particles. They don't have a positive or negative charge. Neutrons help hold the nucleus together. Like protons, neutrons have a mass of one amu.

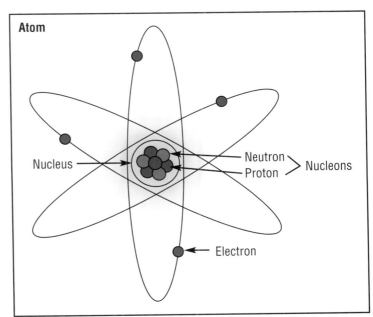

A Nucleus Name

Together, the protons and neutrons are called *nucleons* because they are found in an atom's nucleus.

Electrons are tiny particles that orbit around an atom's nucleus. Electrons are smaller and lighter than protons and neutrons. In fact, their mass is about $1/2000$ of protons and neutrons. Electrons have a negative charge.

Each element usually has the same number of electrons as protons. The positive charges of the protons balance out the negative charges of the electrons, making the atom electrically neutral.

Technology Link

Individually, atoms are too tiny to be seen with the human eye or light microscopes. However, they are visible under the scanning tunneling microscope (STM). The STM was invented in 1981 by German physicist Gerd Binnig and Swiss physicist Heinrich Rohrer. The STM is an electron microscope that's able to produce a 3-D image of a material's surface. It does this by using a very sharp tip located only an atom's thickness above the surface. The tip sends out an electric current, and an electrical signal is received and recorded. STMs have enabled scientists to further study the atom. The microscopes are also used to examine the surfaces of metals for defects and to create tiny electronic devices (nanotechnology). The tip of the STM can actually move atoms around when desired.

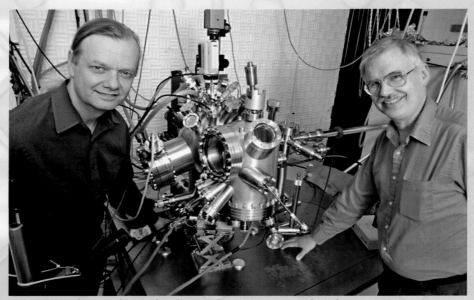

Scientists at the Hewlett-Packard computer company work with an STM.

Electrons Are Elemental

The formation of molecules and compounds depends on electrons. The location and number of electrons in an atom affects how the atom combines with other atoms. Let's take a look at how this works.

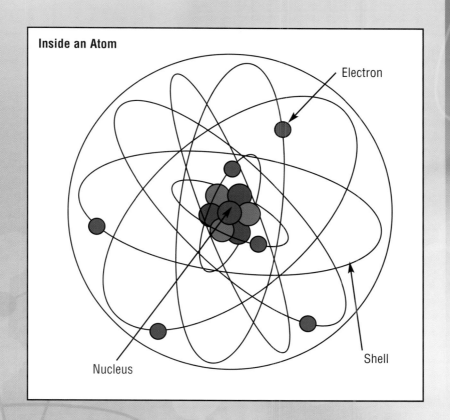

Inside an Atom

Electron

Nucleus

Shell

ENERGETIC ELECTRONS

Scientists imagine that electrons travel in **shells** around the atom's nucleus. These shells are also called *electron shells*, *orbits*, *electron clouds*, or *energy levels*. The shells are numbered or lettered beginning with the shell closest to the nucleus. Each shell is capable of holding a maximum number of electrons. For example, shell 1 (or K) can hold only 2 electrons. Any extra electrons get bumped into the next shell. It's like buying tickets for a concert. The first-row seats are filled first, then the second row, etc. The table below shows the first few shells and the maximum number of electrons each can hold.

Shell	Maximum Number of Electrons
1 or K	2
2 or L	8
3 or M	18 (8 for the first 18 elements)
4 or N	32

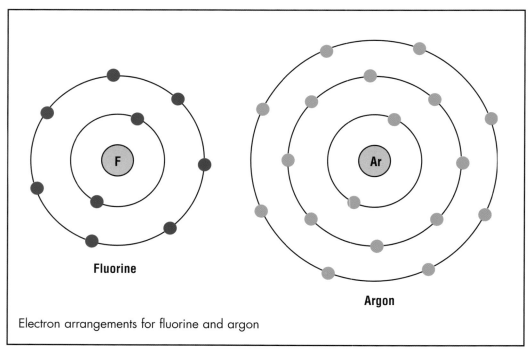

Fluorine

Argon

Electron arrangements for fluorine and argon

Each electron in the same shell has the same amount of energy, so shells are often called *energy levels*. Electrons can leap from one energy level to another. Electrons farther from the nucleus have more energy than ones closer to the nucleus. Atoms need additional energy (for example, heat) for electrons to move from a lower to a higher energy level. Atoms give off energy (for example, light) when electrons move from a higher to a lower level. Electrons can also leap from one atom to another.

ACHIEVING A GOAL

When it comes to forming compounds and molecules, it is useful to think of atoms as having a goal. This goal is to be stable. In general, atoms are stable when their outer shell contains the maximum number of electrons it can hold.

The outermost shell of an atom is its valence shell. The electrons in this shell are called *valence electrons*. These electrons are the key to how elements combine with others to form molecules and compounds because elements tend to join with other elements that can help them complete their outer shells.

Some atoms already have a filled valence shell. Neon, for example, has 10 electrons—2 in its first shell and 8 in its valence shell. This makes neon a very stable element. It does not combine with other elements to form compounds.

Other atoms do not have the maximum number of electrons in their outer shell. They seek to join with other atoms that can help them fill their valence shell. The closer an atom is to having a complete outer shell, the more reactive it tends to be. For example, fluorine has 9 electrons (2 in the first shell and 7 in the second shell). It needs just 1 more electron to fill its valence shell. So fluorine reacts easily with elements, such as sodium and potassium, that have an extra electron to give away.

THE PERIODIC TABLE

Because elements with the same number of valence shell electrons tend to behave the same way, they have been grouped to show these relationships. The periodic table (see page 16) is a common method of organizing the elements.

Scientist of Significance

Dmitri Mendeleev was born in Siberia in 1834. His father died when Dmitri was very young. His mother ran her family's glass factory to provide for her many children. Mendeleev studied hard and became a chemistry teacher and researcher. He worked to improve Russia's technology in agriculture, oil refining, and mining, but he is best known for his development of the modern periodic table in 1869. There were 63 known elements at that time. Previous scientists had organized the elements only by their **atomic weights**. Mendeleev improved on their organization by recognizing patterns in atomic mass and other properties. He went one step further and left certain boxes on the table blank because he predicted that there were undiscovered elements that would complete the pattern. Mendeleev even predicted the elements' properties and weights. His hypothesis was confirmed when future chemists discovered elements having nearly the same properties predicted by Mendeleev. There are now more than 100 known elements in the periodic table.

Each row on the periodic table is called a *period*. All of the elements in each period have atoms with the same number of electron shells. Row 1 elements have 1 shell, row 2 elements have 2 shells, etc. The atoms in each new row have 1 more electron shell than those in the previous row.

Elements with similar chemical properties are located in the same vertical column on the table. These columns are called *groups* (or *families*). They are numbered 1 through 18. All the atoms of elements in a group have the same number of electrons in their valence shells. For example, group 1 atoms have 1 valence electron, and group 17 atoms have 7 valence electrons.

An Exceptional Element
Helium is the one exception to the electron groupings. Helium only has 2 electrons in its outer shell while the other elements in the group have 8. But helium is similar to the other elements in the group because it is stable with only 2 electrons in its outer shell.

GIVE OR TAKE OR SHARE

An element's place on the periodic table provides clues to how it combines with other elements to form compounds. Atoms of certain groups tend to form compounds with atoms of certain other groups. For example, group 1 atoms with 1 valence electron tend to combine with group 17 atoms with 7 valence electrons. Together the atoms can both achieve filled outer shells.

Some atoms combine by giving or taking electrons from each other. Other atoms share electrons to fill their outer shells.

It's Noble to Need Nothing
Group 18 elements already have a filled outer shell, so they don't combine with other elements. These elements are called the *noble gases*. The noble gases include helium, neon, argon, and krypton.

THE PERIODIC TABLE

1 H Hydrogen																		2 He Helium
3 Li Lithium	4 Be Beryllium											5 B Boron	6 C Carbon	7 N Nitrogen	8 O Oxygen	9 F Florine	10 Ne Neon
11 Na Sodium	12 Mg Magnesium											13 Al Aluminum	14 Si Silicon	15 P Phosphorus	16 S Sulfur	17 Cl Chlorine	18 Ar Argon
19 K Potassium	20 Ca Calcium	21 Sc Scandium	22 Ti Titanium	23 V Vanadium	24 Cr Chromium	25 Mn Manganese	26 Fe Iron	27 Co Cobalt	28 Ni Nickel	29 Cu Copper	30 Zn Zinc	31 Ga Gallium	32 Ge Germanium	33 As Arsenic	34 Se Selenium	35 Br Bromine	36 Kr Krypton
37 Rb Rubidium	38 Sr Strontium	39 Y Yttrium	40 Zr Zirconium	41 Nb Niobium	42 Mo Molybdenum	43 Tc Technetium	44 Ru Ruthenium	45 Rh Rhodium	46 Pd Palladium	47 Ag Silver	48 Cd Cadmium	49 In Indium	50 Sn Tin	51 Sb Antimony	52 Te Tellurium	53 I Iodine	54 Xe Xenon
55 Cs Cesium	56 Ba Barium	57 La Lantanum	72 Hf Hafnium	73 Ta Tantalum	74 W Tungsten	75 Re Rhenium	76 Os Osmium	77 Ir Iridium	78 Pt Platinum	79 Au Gold	80 Hg Mercury	81 Tl Thallium	82 Pb Lead	83 Bi Bismuth	84 Po Polonium	85 At Astantine	86 Rn Radon
87 Fr Francium	88 Ra Radium	89 Ac Actinium	104 Rf Unnilquadium	105 Db Unnilpentium	106 Sg Unnilhexium	107 Bh Unnilseptium	108 Hs Unniloctium	109 Mt Unnilennium	110 Uun Ununnilium	111 Uuu Unununium	112 Uub Ununbium						

58 Ce Cerium	59 Pr Praseodymium	60 Nd Neodymium	61 Pm Promethium	62 Sm Samarium	63 Eu Europium	64 Gd Gadolinium	65 Tb Terbium	66 Dy Dysprosium	67 Ho Holmium	68 Er Erbium	69 Tm Thulium	70 Yb Ytterbium	71 Lu Lutetium
90 Th Thorium	91 Pa Protactinium	92 U Uranium	93 Np Neptunium	94 Pu Plutonium	95 Am Americium	96 Cm Curium	97 Bk Berkelium	98 Cf Californium	99 Es Einsteinium	100 Fm Fermium	101 Md Mendelevium	102 No Nobelium	103 Lr Lawrencium

CHAPTER 4

The Name Is Bond . . . Chemical Bond

When atoms take, give, or share electrons to form molecules, how do they stick together? Is there some type of chemical glue holding the atoms together? Actually, molecules are held together by **chemical bonds**. A chemical bond is a force of attraction between atoms that takes energy to create as well as to break. The two most common types of chemical bonds are **ionic bonds** and **covalent bonds**.

IONIC BONDING: PLEASE TAKE IT!

When atoms give or take electrons to complete their outer shell, they form ionic bonds. When an atom gives up electrons or takes electrons from another atom, both atoms become charged. They are then known as **ions**. An ion is an atom with an electric charge. It is no longer neutral.

Salt (NaCl) is a compound held together by ionic bonds.

The element chlorine, for example, has 7 valence electrons. It needs 1 more electron to fill its outer shell. The element sodium, on the other hand, has only 1 valence electron. If it gets rid of that electron, the shell below it will become a filled outer shell. Because each atom needs what the other one has to offer, they bond to form sodium chloride. Since the chlorine took an electron with a negative charge from the sodium, the chlorine is now a negatively charged ion (Cl^{-1}). Since the sodium gave away a negatively charged electron, it is now a positively charged ion (Na^{+1}). The positive charge of the sodium ion (Na^{+1}) is attracted to the negative charge of the chlorine ion (Cl^{-1}). This attraction forms an ionic bond.

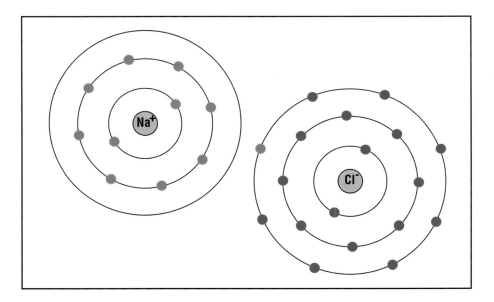

Ionic bonds generally hold inorganic (not containing carbon) materials together. Many rocks and crystals are formed through ionic bonding. Nonmetal atoms also tend to take electrons from metal atoms.

Compounds held together by ionic bonds tend to have high melting points. It takes a lot of heat to change them from a solid to a liquid. Despite this, ionic bonds are generally weaker than other bonds. This means they can be broken more easily. For example, just by mixing it with water, salt can be separated into its sodium and chlorine ions. Ions dissolved in a liquid can conduct electricity.

COVALENT BONDING: CAN WE SHARE?

A covalent bond forms when atoms share their outer electrons with other atoms to complete their valence shells. The electrons zoom around between the two atoms to create the covalent bond. The element carbon, for example, is great at sharing its outer electrons. Carbon has 4 valence electrons. It can form covalent bonds with other carbon atoms to get the 8 electrons it needs to fill its outer shell.

Carbon can also link with atoms of other elements to form covalent compounds. Many fuels are hydrocarbons. Their molecules consist of carbon and hydrogen atoms held together by covalent bonds. Methane, ethane, propane, butane, and benzene are hydrocarbons. When

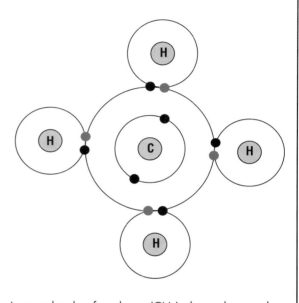

In a molecule of methane (CH_4), the carbon and hydrogen atoms share their outer electrons to complete their valence shells.

oxygen molecules are added to the carbon and hydrogen, covalent compounds such as alcohols, **ethers**, and carbohydrates are formed.

Covalent bonds generally hold **organic** (containing carbon) materials together. Muscle tissue, fat cells, and even DNA is held together by these very strong bonds. Covalent bonds are common between nonmetals. Water (H_2O), carbon dioxide (CO_2), and ammonia (NH_3) are common covalent compounds.

Compounds held together by covalent bonds tend to have low melting points. They change from a solid to a liquid at lower temperatures because there is a very weak attraction between the electrically neutral molecules. Since they don't form ions, covalent compounds also tend not to conduct electricity.

19

Kennett Middle School Library
176 Main St.

Inquire and Investigate: The Melting Points of Ionic and Covalent Compounds

REQUIRES ADULT SUPERVISION

Question: Do ionic or covalent compounds have higher melting points?

Answer the question: I think _____ have higher melting points.

Form a hypothesis: (Ionic or covalent) compounds have higher melting points.

Test the hypothesis:

Materials
- $1/4$ cup of sugar (covalent compound)
- $1/4$ cup of salt (ionic compound)
- frying pan
- stove

Procedure
* Place the frying pan on the stove. Pour the sugar on one side of the pan and the salt on the other side. Cook the sugar and salt over low heat. What happens?

Observations: The sugar melts and the salt doesn't.

Conclusions: Ionic compounds have higher melting points than covalent compounds. That's why the sugar melted but the salt did not. (The salt would not melt even if you cooked it on high. The melting point of salt is nearly 1500°F!)

A BIT OF BOTH BONDS

Most compounds are held together by a combination of bonds. Some atoms in the compound are held together by covalent bonds, while other atoms form ionic bonds. Sodium hydroxide (NaOH) is one example. In this compound, the oxygen and hydrogen are covalently bonded. The oxygen (O) atom needs 2 electrons to complete its outer shell. It gets one of these electrons by sharing the 1 electron in hydrogen's (H) outer shell. This sharing helps the hydrogen fill its outer shell with 2 electrons. The sodium (Na), however, is ionically bonded to the OH molecule. Sodium has one electron in its outer shell, which it gives to the oxygen. This completes the oxygen's outer shell. The sodium now has a filled second shell.

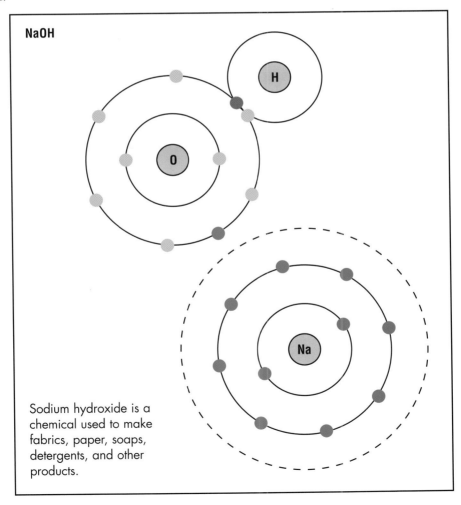

NaOH

Sodium hydroxide is a chemical used to make fabrics, paper, soaps, detergents, and other products.

21

CHAPTER 5

Must-Have Molecules and Compounds

With more than 100 elements and all the possible combinations of atoms, it's almost impossible to imagine all the molecules and compounds that exist—or may someday exist—in the world. A few of these molecules and compounds are essential to your everyday life.

BREATHE IN

Oxygen (O_2) is a simple **diatomic molecule**. All animals, including humans, need oxygen to live. The oxygen is used in cellular respiration. This process breaks down food to release energy and nutrients necessary for survival.

Diatomic Molecules

Diatomic molecules are molecules made up of two atoms of the same type. The two gases—nitrogen and oxygen—that make up most of the air around you are examples of diatomic molecules. One molecule of nitrogen gas (N_2) is made up of two nitrogen atoms. An oxygen gas molecule (O_2) is made up of two oxygen atoms. Hydrogen (H_2), fluorine (F_2), bromine (Br_2), iodine (I_2), and chlorine (Cl_2) are also diatomic molecules.

BREATHE OUT

Carbon dioxide (CO_2) is the gas that animals exhale. It is produced during cellular respiration but is not used by the body. Carbon dioxide is also released during the burning of fuels that contain carbon, such as gasoline in a car or a log on a fire.

Plants use carbon dioxide for photosynthesis. In the presence of sunlight, they change carbon dioxide and water into sugar and oxygen. The plants use the sugar for food and release the oxygen into the air. Animals then take in this oxygen for use in cellular respiration. This carbon dioxide/oxygen cycle is a key element in the interdependence of plants and animals.

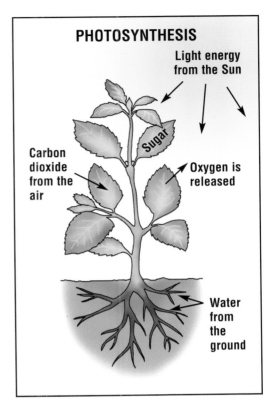

PHOTOSYNTHESIS

Light energy from the Sun

Sugar

Carbon dioxide from the air

Oxygen is released

Water from the ground

TAKE A DRINK

Almost three-fourths of the Earth is covered with water (H_2O). This compound is used for drinking, bathing, washing, and irrigating crops. It is used to make many products that you use on a daily basis. Even the cells that make up all living things are mostly water. Without this important molecule, life would not exist.

GET A LIFE

Certain elements join together to form compounds in living things. The elements carbon, hydrogen, oxygen, nitrogen, phosphorus, and sulfur make up most of these **biomolecules**.

The DNA (deoxyribonucleic acid) that is your genetic code is a huge molecule. DNA is responsible for the formation, growth, and reproduction of individual cells and your entire body. A DNA molecule is shaped like a twisted ladder. It is about five to six feet long when not coiled up inside a human body cell.

A molecule of the sugar glucose is written as $C_6H_{12}O_6$. Glucose is just one type of sugar, but it's an important one to living things. Glucose is the form of sugar made by plants during photosynthesis. Animals also break down glucose to produce energy during cellular respiration.

A model of DNA

The energy produced by cellular respiration in living things is stored in a very important molecule called *adenosine triphosphate (ATP)*. The ATP molecule stores energy until it's needed for chemical reactions within a body's cells. One molecule of glucose can release up to 36 molecules of ATP for energy.

CHAPTER 6

Molecules Made to Order

In addition to the molecules that exist in nature, more than a million molecules have been created in a lab. This work is called *synthetic organic chemistry*. These new molecules are used to make medicines, foods, plastics, clothing, perfumes, high-tech materials, and other products.

COPYCATS

One way chemists can produce molecules is to copy natural compounds made by animals, plants, and bacteria. Many vitamins are copies of natural materials. **Synthetic** vitamin C, for example, can be produced from vegetable carbohydrates. The advantages of human-made vitamins include dosage consistency, purity, and cheaper cost.

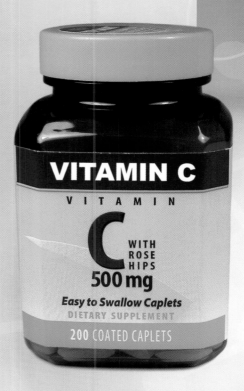

VITAMIN C

VITAMIN

C WITH ROSE HIPS

500 mg

Easy to Swallow Caplets

DIETARY SUPPLEMENT

200 COATED CAPLETS

Another example of reproducing natural compounds is the synthetic drug paclitaxel (Taxol). Taxol is a cancer-fighting medicine. The chemical compound is naturally found in very small amounts in the bark of the Pacific yew tree. Instead of chopping down yew trees to get the compound, scientists can re-create Taxol in a lab using yew needles or a fungus found on the bark of the yew tree.

MADE FROM SCRATCH

Chemists can also create completely new compounds. Plastics are a popular example of this. Plastics are synthetic materials that can be molded or shaped. They are created from organic compounds. Leo Baekeland developed the first synthetic plastic in 1907. It was a hard, moldable plastic called Bakelite. Today, cellophane, garbage bags, rubber, plastic wrap, Teflon, Velcro, vinyl, and even Silly Putty are all forms of plastic.

KEVLAR is another example of a new synthetic compound. Stephanie Kwolek and Herbert Blades, two scientists working for the DuPont Company, created it in 1965. KEVLAR is an incredibly strong

Leo Baekeland

fiber that is resistant to heat. It is also lightweight, flexible, and comfortable. KEVLAR is made into bulletproof vests to protect law enforcement officers. Other products made from KEVLAR include ropes, automotive parts, protective gloves, helmets, hockey sticks, skis, racquets, and kayaks.

KEVLAR fireproof gear

COMPOUNDS CHANGE THE WORLD

Scientists strive to develop molecules and compounds with just the right combination of characteristics to improve life. Added to the millions of materials that nature's elements provide, these molecules and compounds change the world and the way we live in it.

Internet Connections and Related Reading for Atoms, Molecules, and Compounds

http://www.webelements.com/webelements/scholar/index.html
Click on each of the elements in the interactive periodic table to learn more about it.

http://www.chem4kids.com/files/atom_intro.html
This "Chemistry for Kids" site provides an easy-to-understand overview of atoms, elements, ions, compounds, and bonding.

http://www.visionlearning.com/library/module_viewer.php?mid=55
Get a clearer vision of chemical bonding with the information, diagrams, and simulations found here.

http://misterguch.brinkster.net/covalentcompounds.html
How are covalent bonds like ball pits? Find out the answer to this and other questions about covalent bonding at this site.

http://science.howstuffworks.com/atom.htm
Discover more than you probably want to know about how an atom works.

Elements, Compounds and Mixtures by J. M. Patten. A book about what elements, compounds, and mixtures are and how they are useful in everyday life. Rourke Book Company, Inc., 1995. [RL 3 IL 1–3] (0218606 HB)

Matter by Christopher Cooper. This Eyewitness Science Book on matter includes chapters on atoms, compounds, molecules in motion, and designing molecules for specific uses. Dorling Kindersley, 1992. [RL 8.2 IL 3–8] (5869206 HB)

•RL = Reading Level
•IL = Interest Level
Perfection Learning's catalog numbers are included for your ordering convenience. HB indicates hardback.

Glossary

atom (AT uhm) tiny particle that makes up everything in the world

atomic weight (uh TAH mik wayt) average mass of an atom; approximately equal to the sum of an atom's protons and neutrons; also known as atomic mass or relative atomic mass (see separate entries for *proton* and *neutron*)

biomolecule (beye oh MAHL uh kyoul) molecule that makes up living things; molecule produced by or important to a living thing

chemical bond (KEM uh kuhl bahnd) force of attraction that holds atoms and molecules together

chemical reaction (KEM uh kuhl ree AK shuhn) the breaking and forming of chemical bonds to create new substances (see separate entry for *chemical bond*)

compound (KAHM pownd) substance made up of different types of atoms

covalent bond (koh VAY lent bahnd) chemical bond in which the attraction is created by the sharing of electrons (see separate entries for *chemical bond* and *electron*)

diatomic molecule (deye uh TAH mik MAHL uh kyoul) molecule made of two of the same type of atom

electron (ee LEK trahn) negatively charged particle that orbits the nucleus of an atom (see separate entry for *nucleus*)

element (EL uh ment) nonliving material made up of one type of atom

ether (EE ther) compound containing two hydrocarbons linked by an oxygen atom that's found in dyes, waxes, fuels, and anesthesias

ion (EYE ahn) atom that has a positive or negative charge because it has given away or taken one or more electrons

ionic bond (eye AH nik bahnd) chemical bond in which oppositely charged ions are attracted (see separate entries for *chemical bond* and *ion*)

molecule (MAHL uh kyoul) two or more atoms bonded together; smallest unit of a substance that can exist by itself

neutron (NOO trahn) neutral particle found in the nucleus of an atom (see separate entry for *nucleus*)

nucleus (NOO klee uhs) center of an atom that contains the protons and neutrons (see separate entries for *proton* and *neutron*)

organic (or GAN ik) belonging to a family of compounds that contain carbon (see separate entry for *compound*)

proton (PROH tahn) positively charged particle found in an atom's nucleus (see separate entry for *nucleus*)

shell (shel) area around the nucleus where electrons orbit (see separate entries for *electron* and *nucleus*)

synthetic (sin THET ik) artificially made by chemical processes

Index

Kennett Middle School Library
176 Main St.
Conway, NH 03818